AURORA OF AUTHORITY

DECIPHERING THE ENIGMA OF MODERN GEOPOLITICS

Harmonizing the Discordant Symphony of
World Powers

Leo S. Hayes

Copyright © 2024 by Leo S. Hayes.

All rights reserved. No part of this publication may be reproduced, distributed, or transmitted in any form or by any means, including photocopying, recording, or other electronic or mechanical methods, without the prior written permission of the author, except in the case of brief quotations embodied in critical reviews and certain other non-commercial uses permitted by copyright law.

Table of Contents

Introduction 4
Chapter 1 8
The Evolution of Global Power 8
Chapter 2 12
The Rise of New Powers 12
Chapter 3 16
The Unraveling of Traditional Alliances 16
Chapter 4 20
The Digital Revolution and Global Governance 20
Chapter 5 24
Security in a Complex World 24
Chapter 6 28
Economic Power and Influence 28
Chapter 7 32
Cultural Diplomacy and Soft Power 32
Chapter 8 36
Environmental Challenges and Global Governance 36
Chapter 9 40
Human Rights and Global Justice 40
Chapter 10 44
Navigating the Future of Global Power 44
Conclusion 48
About the Author 50

Introduction

Welcome to a journey through the shifting tides of global power. Prepare to embark on an odyssey that will challenge your perceptions, ignite your curiosity, and unveil the intricate tapestry of modern geopolitics.
In the labyrinth of our world's ever-evolving landscape, where titans clash and alliances falter, emerges a phenomenon both enigmatic and awe-inspiring: the Aurora of Authority. Like the ethereal dance of the Northern Lights, this phenomenon casts a luminous glow upon the contours of global influence, illuminating the paths of nations and the destinies of peoples.

As we stand on the precipice of a new era, it is imperative to grasp the profound transformations reshaping our world. The once-stable pillars of international order have begun to tremble, giving way to a kaleidoscope of powers, perspectives, and possibilities. From the ascent of emerging nations to the disruptive forces of digitalization, the contours of global authority are being redrawn before our eyes.

In this book, we embark on a quest to decipher the intricacies of modern geopolitics, guided by the guiding light of the Aurora of Authority. Our journey will take us across continents and centuries, weaving together history, theory, and real-world events to unravel the mysteries of global power dynamics.

But what exactly is the Aurora of Authority? It is more than just a metaphor; it is a concept that encapsulates the essence of our exploration. Just as the aurora illuminates the night sky with its radiant hues, so too does authority cast its glow upon the world stage, shaping the destinies of nations and the lives of billions.

Throughout these pages, we will delve deep into the heart of this phenomenon, seeking to understand its origins, its manifestations, and its implications for the future of humanity. Along the way, we will encounter towering figures of history, navigate treacherous waters of diplomacy, and confront the existential challenges of our time.

But above all, we will embark on a journey of discovery—a journey that will not only enlighten our minds but also ignite our spirits. For in the face of uncertainty and upheaval, it is our quest for knowledge that will guide us forward, illuminating the path to a brighter tomorrow.

So, dear reader, I invite you to join me on this voyage of exploration, as we venture into the heart of the Aurora of Authority and unlock the secrets of modern geopolitics.

Let us set sail together, towards a horizon ablaze with possibility and promise. The adventure begins now.

Chapter 1

The Evolution of Global Power

In the annals of human history, the evolution of global power stands as a testament to the relentless march of progress, ambition, and conquest. From the ancient empires of Mesopotamia to the modern superpowers of the 21st century, the dynamics of global authority have undergone a profound and tumultuous transformation, shaped by the ebb and flow of civilizations, ideologies, and geopolitical rivalries.

At the dawn of recorded history, empires rose and fell with astonishing regularity, each leaving its indelible mark on the fabric of human civilization. From the mighty empires of Rome and Byzantium to the sprawling domains of the Mongols and Ottomans, the world was a tapestry of competing powers vying for supremacy on the global stage. Yet, for all their grandeur and influence, these empires were confined to the boundaries of their time and place, their reach limited by the constraints of geography and communication.

It was not until the dawn of the modern era that the contours of global power began to take shape in ways that would fundamentally reshape the course of human history. The emergence of nation-states in Europe, coupled with the rise of colonial empires and the advent of industrialization, heralded a new era of competition and conflict on a scale never before seen. With the Age of Exploration came the expansion of European influence to every corner of the globe, as empires vied for control of resources, territory, and strategic advantage.

Yet, it was the cataclysm of two world wars in the 20th century that would ultimately reshape the global power landscape in ways that reverberate to this day. The devastation of the First World War shattered the old order of empires and monarchies, giving rise to new ideologies and alliances that would shape the course of the century to come. The emergence of the United States and the Soviet Union as rival superpowers marked the beginning of a new era of bipolarity, characterized by ideological conflict, military buildup, and geopolitical maneuvering on a global scale.

However, the fall of the Berlin Wall in 1989 and the collapse of the Soviet Union signaled the dawn of a new era of unipolarity, with the United States emerging as the sole superpower dominating the global stage. Yet, even as American hegemony seemed unassailable, cracks began to appear in the foundations of the international order, as emerging powers such as China, India, and Brazil asserted their influence and challenged the status quo.

Today, we stand at a crossroads in the evolution of global power, as the forces of globalization, technology, and shifting demographics reshape the contours of international relations. From the rise of non-state actors and transnational networks to the growing influence of regional powers and the resurgence of nationalist movements, the modern geopolitical landscape is a complex and dynamic tapestry of competing interests and conflicting visions of the future.

As we navigate the uncertainties of this new era, it is imperative that we understand the historical forces that have brought us to this point and the key events that continue to shape our world today. From the ancient empires of antiquity to the modern superpowers of the 21st century, the evolution of global power is a story of triumph and tragedy, conquest and collaboration, that continues to unfold before our eyes.

In the pages that follow, we will delve deep into this rich tapestry of human history, tracing the arc of global power from its ancient origins to the complexities of the modern era. Through careful analysis and thoughtful reflection, we will seek to uncover the underlying forces that have shaped the modern geopolitical landscape and explore the challenges and opportunities that lie ahead in our quest to decipher the enigma of global power.

Chapter 2

The Rise of New Powers

In the vast expanse of the global arena, a new constellation of powers has emerged, challenging the traditional dominance of Western nations and reshaping the contours of international relations. At the forefront of this seismic shift are rising giants such as China, India, Brazil, and a host of other emerging economies whose economic prowess and technological innovation have propelled them onto the world stage with unprecedented force.

China, once known as the "Middle Kingdom," has reclaimed its historical position as a global powerhouse, harnessing its vast population and rapid industrialization to become the world's second-largest economy. With a relentless focus on economic growth and technological advancement, China has transformed itself into a modern-day colossus, exerting influence not only in its own backyard but also on a global scale. From its ambitious Belt and Road Initiative to its rapid expansion in areas such as artificial intelligence, renewable energy, and space exploration, China's rise has fundamentally altered the geopolitical landscape, challenging the hegemony of Western powers and sparking a new era of competition and cooperation on the world stage.

India, the world's largest democracy, has likewise emerged as a formidable force in the international arena, leveraging its burgeoning population and burgeoning middle class to drive economic growth and innovation. With a diverse economy spanning industries from IT and telecommunications to pharmaceuticals and renewable energy, India has positioned itself as a key player in the global economy, offering both opportunities and challenges for the established powers of the West. Despite its impressive economic growth, India faces significant hurdles in addressing the needs of its vast and diverse population, raising questions about its ability to sustain its rise to global prominence.

Brazil, the largest country in South America, has also emerged as a rising power on the world stage, driven by its abundant natural resources, agricultural productivity, and growing influence in regional and international affairs. With a rapidly expanding economy and a population of over 200 million people, Brazil has become a key player in global trade and investment, attracting attention from investors and policymakers around the world. However, like China and India, Brazil faces significant challenges, including political instability, corruption, and social inequality, which threaten to undermine its potential as a global leader.

Yet, the rise of these new powers is not without its challenges, as they grapple with the complexities of modern governance, social inequality, and geopolitical rivalries. In China, the authoritarian rule of the Chinese Communist Party has led to concerns about human rights abuses, censorship, and political repression, casting a shadow over its growing influence on the world stage. Similarly, India's democratic credentials have been called into question in recent years, as the country grapples with issues of religious and ethnic tensions, social unrest, and political polarization. In Brazil, corruption scandals and economic instability have raised doubts about the country's ability to realize its full potential as a global leader, highlighting the fragility of its democratic institutions and the challenges of governance in a rapidly changing world.

Moreover, the rise of these new powers poses a fundamental challenge to the traditional dominance of Western nations, whose grip on global power has been shaken by the tides of globalization and technological change. As China and India assert their influence on the world stage, Western powers must confront the reality of a multipolar world order, where their once unassailable dominance is no longer guaranteed. In the face of this shifting geopolitical landscape, Western nations must adapt to new realities and forge new partnerships and alliances to maintain their influence and relevance in an increasingly interconnected world.

Yet, amid the challenges and uncertainties of this new era, there are also opportunities for cooperation and collaboration between East and West, North and South. As the global economy becomes increasingly interconnected, and technological innovation accelerates, the potential for mutual benefit and shared prosperity has never been greater. By embracing the opportunities of globalization and harnessing the power of innovation, nations around the world can work together to address common challenges and build a more inclusive, sustainable, and prosperous future for all.

In the pages that follow, we will delve deep into the rise of these new powers, exploring the economic, political, and technological forces that have propelled them onto the world stage. Through careful analysis and thoughtful reflection, we will seek to understand the implications of their rise for the future of global governance and the balance of power in the 21st century. As we navigate this complex and ever-changing landscape, we must remember that the challenges we face are not insurmountable and that by working together, we can build a better world for future generations to come.

Chapter 3

The Unraveling of Traditional Alliances

In the intricate tapestry of international relations, the fabric of traditional alliances and geopolitical alignments is undergoing a profound and far-reaching transformation. The once-solid bonds of camaraderie and cooperation that defined the post-World War II era are being tested as never before, giving way to a complex web of shifting alliances, strategic rivalries, and geopolitical realignments that defy easy categorization.

At the heart of this unraveling lies a confluence of factors, each contributing to the erosion of traditional alliances and the emergence of new fault lines in the global order. Economic shifts, technological advancements, and changing demographics have all played a role in reshaping the geopolitical landscape, creating both opportunities and challenges for nations around the world.

One of the key drivers of this unraveling is the rise of new economic powers and the decline of traditional economic centers, which has led to a rebalancing of power and influence on the world stage. As emerging economies such as China, India, Brazil, and others assert their economic clout and expand their global reach, established powers in Europe and North America are finding themselves increasingly marginalized, forced to adapt to a new reality in which their once unassailable dominance is no longer assured.

Technological advancements, too, have played a pivotal role in reshaping the geopolitical landscape, enabling new forms of communication, commerce, and conflict that transcend traditional boundaries and alliances. The rise of cyberspace as a domain of warfare and espionage has blurred the lines between friend and foe, creating new challenges for nations seeking to navigate the complexities of modern geopolitics.

Demographic shifts, meanwhile, have brought about changes in the composition of global power and influence, as rising populations in the developing world exert their demographic weight on the international stage. With the world's population expected to reach nearly 10 billion by 2050, the balance of power is shifting inexorably toward regions such as Asia and Africa, where the majority of the world's population resides.

Against this backdrop of change and uncertainty, traditional alliances are being tested as never before, as nations reassess their strategic interests and seek to adapt to a rapidly evolving geopolitical landscape. Case studies from around the world illustrate the changing dynamics of global partnerships, from the fracturing of alliances in Europe to the emergence of new alliances in Asia and beyond.

In Europe, the once-unshakeable bonds of the European Union are being strained by internal divisions and external pressures, as member states grapple with issues such as migration, nationalism, and Brexit. In Asia, meanwhile, the rise of China has led to a reordering of traditional alliances, as countries such as Japan, South Korea, and Australia seek to balance their economic ties with China against their security interests in alliance with the United States.

Yet, amid the turmoil and uncertainty of this new era, there are also opportunities for cooperation and collaboration between nations, as they seek to address common challenges and forge new partnerships for the future. By embracing the complexities of modern geopolitics and working together to find common ground, nations around the world can build a more stable, secure, and prosperous world for generations to come.

In the pages that follow, we will delve deep into the unraveling of traditional alliances, exploring the factors driving this transformation and the implications for the future of international relations. Through careful analysis and thoughtful reflection, we will seek to understand the forces shaping the modern geopolitical landscape and chart a course toward a more harmonious and cooperative world order.

Chapter 4

The Digital Revolution and Global Governance

In the dynamic landscape of international relations, the digital revolution has emerged as a formidable catalyst, reshaping the very fabric of modern geopolitics and challenging entrenched paradigms of governance and sovereignty. As technology continues its relentless march forward, its profound impact on global governance structures and international dynamics becomes increasingly apparent, ushering in an era of unprecedented interconnectedness and complexity that defies conventional boundaries and limitations.

At the core of this transformative upheaval lies the unparalleled power of technology, which has fundamentally transformed the dynamics of how nations interact, communicate, and conduct their affairs on the world stage. From the ubiquitous presence of social media and digital communication platforms to the rapid advancements in artificial intelligence and cyber warfare capabilities, technology has become an omnipresent force shaping the contours of modern geopolitics, exerting influence across a spectrum of diplomatic, economic, and security domains.

A pivotal driver of this digital revolution is the democratization of information and communication, which has empowered individuals and non-state actors to wield unprecedented influence in global affairs. Platforms like Twitter, Facebook, and Instagram have evolved into powerful tools for political mobilization and activism, enabling citizens to rally behind causes, organize mass movements, and amplify their voices on a global scale with unparalleled speed and efficiency.

However, the digital revolution also presents formidable challenges to traditional governance structures and established norms of international relations, as governments and policymakers grapple with the dizzying pace of technological change. The borderless nature of cyberspace has blurred the distinction between domestic and international spheres, creating novel complexities for states seeking to regulate and govern in an increasingly interconnected world.

Furthermore, the rise of digital technologies has given rise to profound questions surrounding privacy, security, and sovereignty in the digital age. The unprecedented accumulation of data by governments and corporations alike raises concerns about individual liberties and the erosion of privacy rights, while the escalating threat of cyber attacks and digital espionage underscores the urgent need for robust cybersecurity measures and enhanced international cooperation to mitigate emerging threats.

Yet, amidst the myriad challenges posed by the digital revolution, there also exists a wealth of opportunities for innovation, collaboration, and progress on the global stage. Digital technologies hold the potential to foster greater transparency, accountability, and efficiency in governance, empowering governments to better serve their citizens and respond adeptly to evolving challenges in real time. From the transformative potential of blockchain technology to the promise of digital identity systems, there exists a vast array of avenues through which technology can be leveraged to foster peace, prosperity, and sustainable development across the globe.

In the ensuing chapters, we will embark on a comprehensive exploration of the digital revolution and its profound implications for global governance and international relations. Through meticulous analysis and nuanced reflection, we will endeavor to unravel the intricate interplay between technology and geopolitics, charting a course toward a more resilient, inclusive, and equitable world order in the digital age.

Chapter 5

Security in a Complex World

In the constantly shifting global landscape, the concept of security has evolved into a multifaceted and intricate tapestry, transcending traditional definitions and demanding a comprehensive understanding of the myriad challenges and threats facing nations worldwide. From the enduring specter of nuclear proliferation and the pervasive threat of terrorism to the insidious rise of cyber warfare and the destabilizing impacts of climate change, the array of security challenges confronting the international community is vast and varied, presenting a complex web of interrelated issues that defy simplistic solutions.

At the heart of these security challenges lies the intricate interplay between traditional state actors and a diverse array of non-state actors, each wielding influence and power in their own distinct ways. While states continue to play a central role in shaping the contours of global security through their military capabilities and diplomatic engagements, non-state actors such as terrorist organizations, criminal networks, and transnational corporations have emerged as formidable players on the world stage, challenging established norms and redefining the boundaries of security in the 21st century.

One of the defining characteristics of the contemporary security landscape is the emergence of a multipolar world order, characterized by the diffusion of power among a diverse array of actors and alliances. In this increasingly complex environment, traditional conceptions of security must be reevaluated and adapted to address the evolving nature of threats and vulnerabilities. From geopolitical rivalries and regional conflicts to transnational crime and global pandemics, the challenges facing the international community are dynamic and multifaceted, requiring innovative and agile responses to effectively manage and mitigate their impacts.

At the same time, the interconnected nature of modern security challenges necessitates a holistic and integrated approach to risk management, one that recognizes the interdependencies between different domains of security and addresses the root causes of insecurity at their source. Strategies for managing security risks in a multipolar world must be flexible, adaptive, and forward-thinking, capable of addressing the underlying drivers of conflict and instability while also responding to the immediate threats posed by violence, extremism, and instability.

In the realm of traditional security, the enduring specter of nuclear proliferation remains a pressing concern, as the proliferation of nuclear weapons and the potential for their use pose a grave threat to global peace and stability. Despite efforts to stem the spread of nuclear weapons through international treaties and diplomatic initiatives, the persistence of nuclear-armed states and the emergence of new nuclear powers continue to undermine efforts to achieve disarmament and non-proliferation goals.

Similarly, the pervasive threat of terrorism continues to loom large in the contemporary security landscape, fueled by a complex web of ideological, political, and socioeconomic factors. From the rise of extremist ideologies to the proliferation of terrorist networks and the exploitation of ungoverned spaces, the challenges posed by terrorism are diverse and multifaceted, requiring a comprehensive and coordinated response from the international community.

In addition to traditional security threats, the advent of the digital age has ushered in a new frontier of security challenges, as the proliferation of information technology and the interconnectedness of cyberspace have created new avenues for exploitation and disruption. From state-sponsored cyber attacks and digital espionage to the spread of disinformation and the manipulation of public opinion, the challenges posed by cyber warfare and information warfare are complex and far-reaching, requiring innovative and adaptive responses from policymakers and practitioners alike.

Furthermore, the destabilizing impacts of climate change are increasingly recognized as a significant security challenge, as rising temperatures, changing weather patterns, and environmental degradation threaten to exacerbate existing tensions and conflicts around the world. From the displacement of populations and the loss of arable land to the disruption of critical infrastructure and the exacerbation of resource scarcity, the security implications of climate change are profound and far-reaching, necessitating a concerted and coordinated global response to mitigate its impacts and build resilience in vulnerable communities.

In the face of these complex and interconnected security challenges, the international community must work together to forge innovative and collaborative solutions that address the root causes of insecurity while also building resilience and fostering cooperation among nations. By embracing a holistic and integrated approach to security, grounded in principles of cooperation, dialogue, and mutual respect, we can confront the challenges of the 21st century with confidence and resilience, forging a more peaceful, prosperous, and secure world for generations to come.

Chapter 6

Economic Power and Influence

In today's multifaceted geopolitical landscape, economic power and influence emerge as pivotal forces, sculpting the conduct of nations and propelling the dynamics of international relations. The global economic order, marked by a nuanced interplay of trade, investment, and financial transactions, stands as both a catalyst for collaboration and a battleground for supremacy among nations striving for dominance in an increasingly interconnected world.

At the core of this global economic order reside several influential players, whose economic might and sway shape the course of global affairs. From the economic giants of the United States and China to the regional juggernauts of the European Union and Japan, these nations command substantial influence over the global economy, dictating market trends, molding trade policies, and propelling economic expansion on a worldwide scale.

The ramifications of trade, investment, and financial activities on geopolitics are profound, blurring the boundaries between domestic and international realms. Trade accords and economic partnerships serve as conduits for economic fusion and collaboration, facilitating the exchange of goods, services, and ideas across borders while nurturing closer bonds between nations.

Similarly, capital flows and financial networks wield significant power in shaping the economic terrain, with multinational corporations and financial institutions exercising influence over national economies and governmental decisions. From foreign direct investment and portfolio allocations to the maneuvers of sovereign wealth funds and hedge funds, the mobility of capital can exert far-reaching effects on geopolitical stability and global economic progress.

A noteworthy trend in the contemporary economic landscape is the ascendance of economic integration and regional cooperation, as nations unite to leverage their collective strengths and resources in tackling shared challenges and advancing common objectives. Regional trade blocs like the European Union and the Association of Southeast Asian Nations (ASEAN), alongside economic alliances such as the Comprehensive and Progressive Agreement for Trans-Pacific Partnership (CPTPP) and the African Continental Free Trade Area

(AfCFTA), have emerged as pivotal drivers of economic dynamism and advancement in the 21st century.

Nonetheless, the global economic order grapples with a myriad of challenges and complexities, as geopolitical frictions and trade disagreements threaten to unsettle the stability and prosperity of the international economic framework. The escalating rivalry between the United States and China, coupled with the resurgence of protectionist measures and nationalist sentiments in certain quarters, casts a shadow over the outlook for global cooperation and economic growth.

In the chapters that ensue, we will embark on an in-depth exploration of the intricate dynamics of economic power and influence in the contemporary world, delving into the complexities and obstacles confronting the global economic order and its ramifications for geopolitics. Through meticulous analysis and reflective examination, we will endeavor to unravel the intricacies of economic integration and regional collaboration, charting a path toward a more resilient, inclusive, and equitable global economy in the 21st century.

Chapter 7

Cultural Diplomacy and Soft Power

In the complex realm of international relations, cultural diplomacy, and soft power emerge as influential forces, shaping perceptions, fostering connections, and wielding significant impact on the global stage. While traditional power dynamics often focus on military might and economic prowess, the potency of culture and soft power lies in their ability to inspire, attract, and persuade, transcending borders and forging bonds between nations and peoples.

Cultural diplomacy, as a strategic tool of statecraft, involves the deliberate promotion of a nation's cultural assets, values, and ideals to enhance its influence and reputation on the world stage. Through initiatives such as cultural exchanges, artistic collaborations, and educational programs, states seek to project a positive image of themselves and build goodwill among foreign populations, thereby fostering mutual understanding and cooperation.

Nonetheless, non-state actors, including cultural institutions, civil society organizations, and grassroots movements, play an increasingly significant role in shaping global perceptions and influencing international relations through cultural diplomacy initiatives. From international film festivals and art exhibitions to music concerts and literary exchanges, these actors leverage cultural expressions as a means of transcending political barriers and fostering dialogue and empathy across diverse communities.

Case studies abound illustrating the effective use of cultural diplomacy by states and non-state actors alike to advance their strategic objectives and enhance their soft power capabilities on the world stage. For instance, countries like France and the United Kingdom have long employed cultural diplomacy as a cornerstone of their foreign policy, leveraging their rich artistic heritage and cultural institutions to project influence and build relationships with other nations.

Similarly, organizations such as UNESCO (United Nations Educational, Scientific and Cultural Organization) play a pivotal role in promoting cultural exchange and dialogue among nations, fostering mutual respect and understanding through initiatives aimed at preserving cultural heritage, promoting linguistic diversity, and fostering creative expression.

In today's interconnected world, where information travels at the speed of light and perceptions can shape political outcomes, the strategic use of cultural assets has become increasingly important for states seeking to enhance their global influence and soft power capabilities. By harnessing the power of culture, nations can transcend traditional barriers and connect with audiences on a deeper, more emotional level, fostering goodwill and cooperation on the world stage.

Strategies for leveraging cultural assets to enhance global influence encompass a range of approaches, from investing in cultural infrastructure and promoting cultural exchange programs to supporting the creative industries and harnessing digital technologies to reach global audiences. By investing in cultural diplomacy initiatives that promote dialogue, foster understanding, and celebrate diversity, nations can enhance their soft power capabilities and cultivate lasting relationships with partners around the world.

In the chapters ahead, we will delve deeper into the role of culture and soft power in international relations, examining the strategic implications of cultural diplomacy and exploring the ways in which nations and non-state actors leverage their cultural assets to enhance their global influence and shape the contours of the contemporary world order. Through rigorous analysis and critical reflection, we will seek to unravel the complexities of cultural diplomacy and chart a course toward a more inclusive and interconnected world, where the power of culture serves as a force for positive change and cooperation on the global stage.

Chapter 8

Environmental Challenges and Global Governance

In the ever-evolving landscape of global affairs, environmental challenges have emerged as pressing issues with far-reaching implications for geopolitics and international relations. From climate change and biodiversity loss to pollution and resource depletion, these challenges pose significant threats to the stability and security of nations around the world, underscoring the interconnectedness of human societies and the natural environment.

The analysis of environmental threats requires a comprehensive understanding of their multifaceted nature and the complex interactions between human activities and ecological systems. Climate change, driven primarily by greenhouse gas emissions from human activities such as burning fossil fuels and deforestation, poses one of the most significant challenges of our time, with potentially catastrophic consequences for ecosystems, economies, and societies worldwide.

Moreover, biodiversity loss, driven by habitat destruction, overexploitation of natural resources, and the spread of invasive species, threatens the resilience of ecosystems and the services they provide, from food and water security to climate regulation and disease control. Pollution, including air and water pollution, soil contamination, and plastic waste, further exacerbates environmental degradation, posing health risks to human populations and ecosystems alike.

In response to these environmental challenges, the international community has undertaken concerted efforts to address climate change, biodiversity loss, and other pressing environmental issues through multilateral agreements and global governance mechanisms. The landmark Paris Agreement, adopted in 2015 under the auspices of the United Nations Framework Convention on Climate Change (UNFCCC), represents a historic commitment by nearly 200 countries to limit global warming to well below 2 degrees Celsius above pre-industrial levels and to pursue efforts to limit the temperature increase to 1.5 degrees Celsius.

Similarly, international initiatives such as the Convention on Biological Diversity (CBD), the United Nations Environment Programme (UNEP), and the Intergovernmental Panel on Climate Change (IPCC) play pivotal roles in advancing scientific research, fostering cooperation among nations, and promoting sustainable development practices worldwide. These efforts aim to mitigate the impacts of environmental degradation, build resilience to climate change, and promote the conservation and sustainable use of natural resources for the benefit of present and future generations.

However, despite these efforts, significant challenges remain in translating international commitments into meaningful action on the ground. The Paris Agreement, while a landmark achievement in international climate diplomacy, faces implementation challenges and requires enhanced ambition and collaboration among nations to achieve its goals. Similarly, the Convention on Biological Diversity has yet to achieve its targets for biodiversity conservation and sustainable development, highlighting the need for greater political will and financial resources to address the root causes of environmental degradation.

Moreover, the COVID-19 pandemic has exposed vulnerabilities in global governance systems and underscored the interconnectedness of human health, economic prosperity, and environmental sustainability. As nations strive to recover from the socio-economic impacts of the pandemic, there is a growing recognition of the need to build back better and to pursue a more sustainable and resilient path to development that respects planetary boundaries and promotes inclusive and equitable growth.

In the chapters ahead, we will delve deeper into the complex interplay between environmental challenges and geopolitics, examining the implications of climate change, biodiversity loss, and other environmental issues for international security, economic development, and social stability. Through rigorous analysis and critical reflection, we will explore the role of global governance mechanisms in promoting sustainability and resilience, charting a course toward a more sustainable and prosperous future for all.

Chapter 9

Human Rights and Global Justice

In the intricate landscape of global affairs, the promotion and protection of human rights stand as indispensable principles, serving as pillars of justice and dignity in the international arena. However, amid the complex dynamics of geopolitical power, human rights challenges persist, casting shadows over the ideals enshrined in international law and norms. In this chapter, we embark on a nuanced exploration of human rights within the context of global power dynamics, analyzing the intricate interplay between geopolitics and the pursuit of justice on a global scale.

At the core of the human rights discourse lies the recognition of the inherent dignity and worth of every individual, irrespective of their race, ethnicity, gender, religion, or nationality. Yet, in the pursuit of power and influence on the world stage, nations often find themselves entangled in webs of oppression, discrimination, and injustice, perpetuating cycles of violence and inequality that undermine the very essence of humanity.

Against this backdrop, international efforts to uphold human rights and justice play a pivotal role in advancing the cause of universal dignity and equality. Through the adoption of landmark treaties, conventions, and declarations, as well as the establishment of specialized institutions and mechanisms, the global community has made significant strides in codifying and safeguarding fundamental human rights. These include the rights to life, liberty, and security of person; freedom of expression and assembly; and protection against torture, discrimination, and arbitrary detention.

However, despite these advancements, human rights violations continue to persist in various forms and contexts, fueled by political repression, armed conflict, socioeconomic disparities, and cultural intolerance. From the persecution of political dissidents and journalists to the systematic discrimination against marginalized communities and the brutal suppression of peaceful protests, violations of human rights remain prevalent across the globe, challenging the principles of justice, equality, and democracy.

Throughout this chapter, we delve into the intricate dynamics of human rights within the context of global power dynamics, examining how geopolitical considerations influence the promotion and protection of human rights on the world stage. Through rigorous analysis and critical reflection, we explore the intersection of geopolitics and human rights, unraveling the underlying drivers of human rights abuses and evaluating the effectiveness of international efforts to address them.

Illustrative case studies from diverse regions and contexts provide valuable insights into the complex interplay between political power, economic interests, and human rights considerations. From the plight of refugees and asylum seekers fleeing conflict and persecution to the struggles of indigenous communities fighting for land rights and environmental justice, these case studies shed light on the challenges and opportunities inherent in the pursuit of global justice.

Moreover, we examine the roles of key actors and institutions in advancing the cause of human rights and justice on the world stage. From national governments and international organizations to civil society groups and grassroots movements, a diverse array of stakeholders play crucial roles in shaping the global discourse on human rights and holding perpetrators of abuses accountable.

In conclusion, this chapter offers a thought-provoking analysis of human rights within the context of global power dynamics, challenging readers to confront the complexities and contradictions inherent in the quest for global justice. Through a nuanced examination of the intersection of geopolitics and human rights, we aim to deepen our understanding of the challenges and opportunities facing the international community in promoting a world where the inherent dignity and rights of all individuals are respected and protected.

Chapter 10

Navigating the Future of Global Power

In contemplating the forthcoming trajectory of global power dynamics, it becomes imperative to introspect on the pivotal trends and challenges that are molding the evolving landscape of geopolitics. As we stand at the brink of a new epoch characterized by rapid technological advancements, shifting demographic patterns, and geopolitical realignments, it is imperative for policymakers, practitioners, and citizens alike to navigate these complexities with foresight, resilience, and a commitment to collective action.

One of the defining trends of the 21st century is the continued ascent of emerging powers and the rebalancing of global influence. Nations such as China, India, Brazil, and others are asserting themselves on the world stage, challenging the traditional dominance of Western powers and reshaping the contours of international relations. As these emerging powers endeavor to carve out their place in the global order, they bring with them novel perspectives, priorities, and aspirations, which will inevitably mold the future trajectory of geopolitics.

Simultaneously, the world is grappling with a plethora of intricate challenges, from climate change and environmental degradation to the ascent of transnational terrorism and the proliferation of weapons of mass destruction. These challenges transcend national borders and necessitate collective action at the international level. However, the existing mechanisms of global governance are often insufficient to address these issues effectively, hindered by geopolitical rivalries, institutional inertia, and a dearth of political will.

In navigating the future of global power, it is imperative for policymakers to embrace a forward-thinking approach that prioritizes cooperation, inclusivity, and sustainability. This necessitates fostering dialogue and collaboration among nations, harnessing the power of multilateral institutions, and investing in the development of innovative solutions to pressing global challenges.

Furthermore, it is incumbent upon practitioners across various sectors – including diplomacy, development, and security – to adapt to the evolving geopolitical landscape and embrace innovative approaches to problem-solving. This may entail building bridges across divides, fostering trust and mutual understanding, and seeking common ground on shared interests and objectives.

For citizens, the future of global power presents both opportunities and responsibilities. In an increasingly interconnected world, individual actions can have far-reaching consequences, whether through advocacy, activism, or everyday choices. By engaging with global issues, holding leaders accountable, and advocating for positive change, citizens can play a vital role in shaping the future trajectory of geopolitics and advancing the cause of peace, justice, and sustainability.

In summation, the future of global power is a complex and multifaceted realm, shaped by a myriad of intersecting trends and challenges. Yet, amidst the uncertainties and complexities, there also lies the potential for positive transformation and progress. By embracing a forward-thinking mindset, fostering collaboration and innovation, and committing to the values of inclusivity, sustainability, and peace, we can navigate the future of global power with confidence and optimism, forging a path toward a more equitable, resilient, and prosperous world for generations to come.

Conclusion

As we draw the curtains on this exploration of contemporary geopolitics, it is incumbent upon us to reflect on the key insights and findings gleaned from our journey through the intricate tapestry of global power dynamics. Throughout the chapters, we have delved deep into the complexities and nuances of the modern geopolitical landscape, unpacking the interplay of political, economic, social, and technological forces that shape the behavior of nations and drive the dynamics of international relations.

From the rise of emerging powers to the challenges of global governance, from the impacts of environmental degradation to the imperatives of human rights and justice, our exploration has offered a panoramic view of the multifaceted challenges and opportunities that define the modern era. We have witnessed the evolution of traditional power structures, the emergence of new actors and alliances, and the increasing interconnectedness of the global community.

At the heart of this endeavor lies the recognition of the critical importance of understanding and engaging with global power dynamics in an increasingly interconnected and interdependent world. As citizens of this global community, we bear a collective responsibility to navigate the complexities of the modern geopolitical landscape with wisdom, foresight, and a commitment to shared values and principles.

Indeed, the challenges we face – whether in the realms of security, economics, environment, or human rights – are daunting, but they are not insurmountable. By fostering dialogue, cooperation, and collaboration among nations, by investing in the development of innovative solutions and institutions, and by harnessing the power of collective action, we can chart a course towards a more inclusive, sustainable, and peaceful world order.

As we conclude this journey, I extend a heartfelt call to all readers to continue exploring and contributing to the discourse on geopolitics. Whether through further study, informed debate, or active engagement in civic and political life, each of us has a role to play in shaping the future trajectory of global affairs. Let us seize this opportunity with courage, compassion, and a commitment to building a better world for ourselves and future generations.

About the Author

Leo S. Hayes is an esteemed scholar and seasoned analyst with a passion for unraveling the complexities of global geopolitics. With a rich background in international relations, political science, and strategic studies, Hayes brings a wealth of knowledge and expertise to his work, offering unique insights into the intricate dynamics of the modern world.

Throughout his career, Hayes has dedicated himself to the study of global power dynamics, exploring the intersections of politics, economics, security, and culture in shaping the behavior of nations and the course of international relations. His research spans a wide range of topics, from the rise of emerging powers to the challenges of environmental sustainability, from the promotion of human rights to the imperatives of global governance.

As a prolific writer and thought leader, Hayes has authored numerous articles, essays, and research papers, delving into the complexities of contemporary geopolitics and offering innovative solutions to the challenges facing the international community. His work is characterized by its depth of analysis, clarity of thought, and commitment to advancing the cause of peace, justice, and prosperity in an increasingly interconnected world.

In addition to his academic pursuits, Hayes is also deeply engaged in policy advocacy and public discourse, lending his expertise to government agencies, international organizations, and civil society groups seeking to address global challenges and promote global cooperation. He is a frequent speaker at conferences, seminars, and workshops, where his insights and perspectives are eagerly sought after by policymakers, practitioners, and scholars alike.

Hayes holds advanced degrees in international relations and political science from leading universities, where he received numerous accolades and awards for his academic achievements. He continues to be actively involved in research, teaching, and mentorship, inspiring the next generation of scholars and practitioners to engage critically and constructively with the complexities of global affairs.

In his spare time, Hayes enjoys traveling, hiking, and exploring different cultures and cuisines. He is a firm believer in the power of dialogue, empathy, and mutual understanding to bridge divides and build a more peaceful and prosperous world for all. Through his work and his example, Hayes strives to make a meaningful and lasting contribution to the pursuit of global peace and security.

www.ingramcontent.com/pod-product-compliance
Lightning Source LLC
Chambersburg PA
CBHW050244230526
45470CB00005B/2110